MISSING

Sarah Hutt

SADDLEBACK
EDUCATIONAL PUBLISHING

ASTONISHING HEADLINES

Attacked

Captured

Condemned

Kidnapped

Lost and Found

Missing

Shot Down

Stowed Away

Stranded at Sea

Trapped

SADDLEBACK
EDUCATIONAL PUBLISHING
www.sdlback.com

Copyright © 2005, 2013 by Saddleback Educational Publishing
All rights reserved. No part of this book may be reproduced in any form or by any means, electronic or mechanical, including photocopying, recording, scanning, or by any information storage and retrieval system, without the written permission of the publisher. SADDLEBACK EDUCATIONAL PUBLISHING and any associated logos are trademarks and/or registered trademarks of Saddleback Educational Publishing.

ISBN-13: 978-1-61651-923-0
ISBN-10: 1-61651-923-1
eBook: 978-1-61247-080-1

Printed in Guangzhou, China
0712/CA21201055

17 16 15 14 13   1 2 3 4 5

Photo Credits: page 17, NY Photo Press; page 35, NASA; page 59, Larry Lipsky, Index Stock Imagery; pages 68–69, William Vandivert / Time & Life Pictures / Getty Images; pages 74–75, © Jaime Pharr | Dreamstime.com; pages 80–81, © Aaron Rutten | Dreamstime.com

CONTENTS

INTRODUCTION

Missing. Lost. Gone without a trace. No clues. Sometimes, only a mystery remains. Have you ever had your favorite CD or shirt go missing? You might get mad or annoyed looking for it. But what happens when a real treasure goes missing, or a space ship, or a person? Missing persons leave behind anxious and terrified loved ones.

Missing criminals are fugitives on the run from the law. They might have been captured by police officers, but then escaped. Or they might be suspects on the run, trying to avoid arrest. For crime fighters, it is very important to find missing criminals and make sure they are not a danger to the public.

It can be very sad, scary, or tragic when something important goes missing. Whole ships have vanished without a trace. Entire species of animals or plants can vanish from Earth. At first glance, it can seem as if there are no clues. But determined detectives and scientists look for answers.

Some of these disappearances have puzzled experts for years. With very few clues, they have to work out what exactly happened. Some of these disappearances are solved through detective work and luck. Others remain mysteries, never to be solved.

The FBI's Ten Most Wanted
DATAFILE

Timeline

July 1908

Theodore Roosevelt creates the FBI.

March 1950

FBI creates the "Ten Most Wanted Fugitives" list.

June 1999

Terrorist Osama bin Laden is added to the FBI's
Ten Most Wanted list.

Where is Washington, DC?

HERE

Key Terms

database—a computerized list of information

federal—having to do with the U.S. government

parole—a closely watched prisoner on release from jail

terrorist—a person who tries to attack a country or group using violence

?

Did You Know?

Only seven women have made the FBI's Ten Most Wanted list. The first was Ruth Eisemann-Schier. Eisemann-Schier was wanted for kidnapping a Miami heiress in Decatur, Georgia. Eisemann-Schier later demanded $500,000 ransom for her safe return.

The FBI's Ten Most Wanted

What is the FBI?

FBI stands for Federal Bureau of Investigation. The FBI captures people who break federal laws. Federal laws are those that apply to the country as a whole, not just to a single city or state.

The FBI also finds criminals who cross state lines. If a criminal commits crimes in more than one state, his or her crimes become a national concern. This is when the FBI helps local and state police catch the criminals.

The FBI also protects the United States from international criminals. International criminals are people who live in the United States, but commit crimes in other countries. There are also foreign criminals, such as terrorists, who target the United States.

FBI Beginnings

President Theodore Roosevelt created the FBI in July 1908. In the FBI's early days, there were very few federal crimes. Investigators spent most of their time tracking down stolen goods and solving bank robberies. Capturing high-profile fugitives did not become important for the FBI until the 1950s.

J. Edgar Hoover became the director of the FBI in 1924, when he was only 29 years old. He set out to enlarge the FBI's role as a crime-fighting organization. Hoover introduced new programs, some of which are still used by the FBI today.

In 1926, Hoover started a fingerprint file. Fingerprints are used to help identify criminals. This file turned into one of the largest fingerprint databases in the world.

Toughest Criminals

Hoover's other important idea was the FBI's Ten Most Wanted list. This list is an important crime-fighting tool. It is still used today.

The FBI's Ten Most Wanted Fugitives is a list of the 10 fugitives the FBI wants to catch the most. The list includes the name, a description, and a picture of each criminal. It also tells why the criminal is wanted. The list's purpose is to keep the public on the lookout for criminals on the run.

The idea came about when a reporter named Sam Fogg called the FBI one day in 1949.

Sam worked for the International News Service. He did not have any breaking news to report, so he decided to find out what or whom the FBI was investigating. He asked the FBI for the name and description of the 10 "toughest guys" they were tracking.

Fogg went on to write stories about these men for the news service. As a result, two of the men on the list were caught. Hoover realized the success of this idea and created a permanent list of the Ten Most Wanted Fugitives in March 1950.

The First Catch

The first person on the list was Thomas J. Holden. He was convicted of robbery and sent to prison. After many years in jail, he was released on parole. While Holden was free, he shot and killed his wife and her two brothers. Then he went on the run.

The FBI put his picture on the list. Back then, the Ten Most Wanted list was posted in post offices, general stores, and newspapers.

In June 1951, an Oregon resident spotted Holden. He was working under a different name. The resident told the FBI and Holden was captured.

The number of fugitives appearing on the FBI's Ten Most Wanted List continues to grow. But the number of those found and arrested increases as well—many due to help from the public.

Today's Ten Most Wanted

In the 1950s, most of the criminals on the list were bank robbers, car thieves, and murderers. As the times changed, so did the types of criminals on the list.

Over the years, the list has included gangsters, drug dealers, and terrorists. Criminals are put on the list because they have a history of committing serious crimes, or they are very dangerous. Criminals are removed from the list only if they are captured or no longer considered dangerous. When a fugitive is taken off the list, the FBI adds a new one. The FBI only lists criminals they think will be caught by showing them to the public. High-profile criminals in the news usually do not make the list.

America's Most Wanted

In July 1981, John Walsh's six-year-old son, Adam, was abducted and killed. John Walsh and his wife were very sad about their son's death. They decided to try and stop criminals from hurting other people. They started the television program *America's Most Wanted* in 1987.

The show broadcasts pictures and information about America's most-wanted criminals. TV viewers can call in and report criminals if they spot them on the street. The show has been very successful in helping law enforcement capture wanted fugitives.

Famous Cases, Funny Names

Bank robberies and police shootouts with gangsters were the crimes of the 1920s to 1950s. Here are some famous FBI cases.

"Baby Face" Nelson

"Baby Face" Nelson was called "Baby Face" due to his young appearance. Nelson was wanted for the murder of five FBI agents, armed robbery, and auto theft in a crime spree from1922–1934.

Charles A. "Pretty Boy" Floyd

"Pretty Boy" Floyd was wanted for his part in The Kansas City Massacre in 1933, in which five men died. Floyd was a bank robber and a murderer.

George "Machine Gun" Kelley

"Machine Gun" Kelley was wanted by the FBI for kidnapping wealthy businessman, Charles F. Urschel in 1933.

THE FBI'S MOST NOTORIOUS WANTED CRIMINAL

OSAMA BIN LADEN

- Aliases: Usama bin Muhammad bin Ladin, Shaykh Usama bin Ladin, the Prince, the Emir, Abu Abdallah, Mujahid Shaykh, Hajj, the Director
- Date of Birth: 1957
- Hair: Brown
- Place of Birth: Saudi Arabia
- Eyes: Brown
- Height: 6' 4" to 6' 6"
- Complexion: Olive
- Weight: 160 pounds
- Sex: Male
- Build: Thin
- Nationality: Saudi Arabian
- Occupation: Unknown
- Scars and Marks: None
- Bin Laden was the leader of the terrorist group al-Qaeda, "The Base." He was left handed and walked with a cane.

FBI TEN MOST WANTED FUGITIVE

MURDER OF U.S. NATIONALS OUTSIDE THE UNITED STATES;
CONSPIRACY TO MURDER U.S. NATIONALS OUTSIDE THE UNITED STATES;
ATTACK ON A FEDERAL FACILITY RESULTING IN DEATH

USAMA BIN LADEN

Date of Photograph Unknown

Aliases: Usama Bin Muhammad Bin Ladin, Shaykh Usama Bin Ladin, the Prince, the Emir, Abu Abdallah, Mujahid Shaykh, Hajj, the Director

DESCRIPTION

Date of Birth:	1957	**Hair:**	Brown
Place of Birth:	Saudi Arabia	**Eyes:**	Brown
Height:	6' 4" to 6' 6"	**Complexion:**	Olive
Weight:	Approximately 160 pounds	**Sex:**	Male
Build:	Thin	**Nationality:**	Saudi Arabian
Occupation(s):	Unknown		
Remarks:	He is the leader of a terrorist organization known as Al-Qaeda "The Base." He walks with a cane.		

CAUTION

USAMA BIN LADEN IS WANTED IN CONNECTION WITH THE AUGUST 7, 1998, BOMBINGS OF
THE UNITED STATES EMBASSIES IN DAR ES SALAAM, TANZANIA AND NAIROBI, KENYA.
THESE ATTACKS KILLED OVER 200 PEOPLE.

CONSIDERED ARMED AND EXTREMELY DANGEROUS

IF YOU HAVE ANY INFORMATION CONCERNING THIS PERSON, PLEASE CONTACT YOUR
LOCAL FBI OFFICE OR THE NEAREST U.S. EMBASSY OR CONSULATE.

REWARD

The United States Government is offering a reward of up to $5 million for information leading directly
to the apprehension or conviction of Usama Bin Laden.

www.fbi.gov

May 1999

Bin Laden's wanted poster. He was killed by US Navy SEALs in 2011.

CHAPTER 2

The Bermuda Triangle
DATAFILE

Timeline

December 1944

Flight 19 disappears over the Bermuda Triangle.

February 1960

Journalist Vincent H. Gaddis makes up the name "Bermuda Triangle."

Where is the Bermuda Triangle?

Key Terms

compass—a magnetic tool that points to the direction you are heading

magnetic north—the northerly direction of Earth's magnetic north pole

phenomenon—an amazing or hard to explain event

portal—a door or entrance; a way in or out

supernatural—beyond natural or scientific forces

true north—the direction of the North Pole

vessels—boats, ships

?

Did You Know?

The "Devil's Sea" is the only place other than the Bermuda Triangle where compasses point to true north. The "Devil's Sea" is off Japan's east coast.

The Bermuda Triangle

The Bermuda Triangle is an area of the Atlantic Ocean covered in mystery. Also called "The Devil's Triangle," this spot has been the site of many disappearances. Since the 1900s, more than 50 ships and 20 planes have gone missing in the Bermuda Triangle. Many of these boats and planes just vanished. They made no distress calls and left no wreckage behind.

The Bermuda triangle is a stretch of water that forms a triangle between eastern Florida, the islands of Bermuda, and Puerto Rico. The triangle is more than 500,000 square miles in size. For some, crossing the triangle can be a scary experience because of the mystery that surrounds it.

Over time, the mystery of the missing ships and planes led many people to believe supernatural forces were at work in the triangle.

Flight 19

One of the most famous Bermuda Triangle mysteries is the disappearance of Flight 19. Flight 19 was a squadron of five Avenger torpedo bombers. On December 5, 1944, the planes left the Fort Lauderdale Florida Naval Air Station at 2:00 p.m. It was a training mission with a team of 13 students and one commander.

At around 3:00 p.m., the commander radioed to say his compass had stopped working. He believed he was close to Florida. But actually, the team was really headed in a different direction. They continued to fly further out into the ocean.

By nightfall, the team did not know where they were and had also lost radio contact. The weather was getting bad and the planes were low on fuel.

Three other planes were sent out to look for Flight 19. Among them was a Martin Mariner. By the next morning, not only was Flight 19 missing, but the Martin Mariner had disappeared as well.

What Happened to Flight 19?

Historians believe that Flight 19's crew simply got lost. The commander did not realize the difference in his compass readings in the Bermuda Triangle. He steered the planes out into the ocean until they were lost. They got too far out to communicate by radio.

Experts believe the planes ran out of fuel, and then crashed into the ocean. The heavy iron planes instantly sank to the ocean floor and were swept away.

Many people believe the Martin Mariner airplane that searched for Flight 19 blew up. These planes were known to leak fuel when they were flying. Sailors at sea saw an explosion right after the Mariner took off from Banana River Naval Air Station.

It is very likely that one of the passengers on the plane lit a cigarette. The plane, full of fumes, instantly blew up. It sank and was never found.

Supernatural Stories

Over the years, many other ships and planes have sailed or flown off into the Bermuda Triangle, never to be seen again. All kinds of spectacular stories try to explain the Bermuda Triangle's phenomenon.

These stories include a giant octopus that attacks planes and sinks ships. Another idea is that aliens built a portal to another dimension in the triangle. This portal supposedly opens 25 times a year and transports ships and planes to another world where they stay trapped in space and time.

However, scientists and experts have worked hard to explain away these legends. Scientists believe there are scientific reasons why so many ships and planes go down in this area.

What's in a Name?

The "Bermuda Triangle," is not recognized as an official name for this mysterious stretch of ocean. A journalist named Vincent H. Gaddis made up the name for an article in the magazine "Argosy" in February 1964. The article was about the strange number of disappearances in the area.

Gaddis's article got people interested in the Bermuda Triangle's mysteries. It also helped spread the spooky legends surrounding the Bermuda Triangle.

The Real Story

The Bermuda Triangle is one of two places in the world where compasses point to the North Pole, or true north. Usually compasses point to magnetic north. Navigators adjust their steering because of the difference in true north and magnetic north. But if they do this in the Bermuda Triangle, they will head in the wrong direction and get lost.

The Bermuda Triangle is also known for quick changes in weather. Warm tropical air from the islands constantly bumps into colder air from the United States. This causes flash storms, waterspouts, and dangerous traveling conditions.

Finally, sailor and pilot error is always a possibility. Accidents can happen without warning. The Bermuda Triangle is a busy part of the ocean. Because there are many ships in this area, there are bound to be accidents. The Bermuda Triangle's strong currents also sweep shipwrecks away into deep holes in the ocean floor. When ships sink in the Bermuda Triangle, they truly are gone without a trace.

Scientists and historians challenge themselves to solve supernatural events with logical explanations. If the wrecks are found, they will have evidence to prove their theories. As long as these vessels remain missing, we can never really know what happened.

Disappearances

With the use of advanced GPS (Global Positioning System) technology, not many ships have gone missing. But some ships and planes are believed to be lost in the Bermuda Triangle in recent years.

- 1994, December 25: plane missing over Florida; pilot lost.

- 1995, March 20: boat: *Jamanic K.* missing on route from Haiti to Miami.

- 1996, May 2: Atlantic/Caribbean charter plane missing with three aboard.

- 1996, October 14: boat: Intrepid missing 30 miles off Fort Pierce, FL; 16 aboard.

- 1997, December: boat: *Robalo* missing off Virginia Beach.

- 1998, January 2: boat: *Grumpy* found derelict.

- 1998, May 1: boat: *Miss Charlotte* hit by a force that sucked everything off deck, then sunk; crew survived. Thought to be a water spout; off North Carolina coast.

- 1998, August 10: boat: *Erica Lynn* missing.

- 1998, August 19: Atlantic/Caribbean charter plane missing; 4 aboard.

- 1998, November: boat: *Carolina* missing off Cape May coast.

- 1998, November: boat: *Interlude* disappeared during cruise to Cayman Islands.

- 1999, April 15: boat: *Miss Fernandina* missing off Flagler Beach, FL.; last signaled: net caught in propeller, electrical drain, listing.

- 1999, April 23: boat: *Genesis* sailed from Port of Spain.

- 1999, May 12, plane missing near Nassau, Bahamas; pilot aboard.

- 1999, August 5: boat: Unknown name found derelict except for the dog; off North Carolina coast.

- 1999, November 15: boat: Unknown name missing between Frying Pan Shoals and Frying Pan Light, North Carolina; 2 aboard.

- 1999, December 27, boat: *Alyson Selene* found derelict 7 miles northeast of Andros, Bahamas.

- 2000, April, freighter: *Gran Rio R* disappears off West Indies coast.

- 2000, August 14, boat: *Hemmingway* is found deserted; missing crew and captain.

- 2001, June 22, boat: *Tropic Bird* is found derelict off Antigua.

- 2001, October 27, plane missing after leaving Winterhaven, FL; pilot aboard.

- 2002, September 23, freighter: *Fiona R* missing off West Indies en route to St. Vincent.

- 2003, November 25, boat: *Peanuts Too* is found deserted south of Bermuda.

- 2003, September 6, plane missing southeast of Nassau, Bahamas; pilot aboard

CHAPTER 3

Mission to Mars
DATAFILE

Timeline

July and September 1976

Viking 1 and *Viking 2* land on Mars.

July 1988

Phobos I and *Phobos II* travel to Mars.

July 1997

Pathfinder lands on Mars.

Where is Mars?

HERE

Key Terms

astronomer—a scientist who studies Earth, planets, stars, and space

NASA—National Aeronautics and Space Administration: the team that runs the U.S. space program

orbit—to move about something in a circular path

telescope—an instrument for viewing distant objects by refracting light rays through a lens or the reflection of light rays by a concave mirror

?

Did You Know?

Mars has two moons orbiting the planet. They are called Phobos and Deimos. *Phobos* is Greek for "fear." *Deimos* is Greek for "panic."

Mission to Mars

The planet Mars is Earth's closest neighbor. Mars is also called the Red Planet. Early stargazers noticed the color and thought it looked like blood. Because of this they named the planet after Mars, the Roman god of war. Its red color is due to rusting metal particles on the planet's surface.

With the invention of the telescope, early astronomers got a better look at Mars. In the late 1800s, an astronomer named Percival Lowell thought he could see canals on Mars's surface. Lowell believed that intelligent life forms must have built them.

As telescopes improved, astronomers saw that there were no canals on Mars. However, the idea that Martians might live on the planet interested scientists and thrilled people.

Today, scientists have made great progress in trying to answer the question: "Is there life on Mars?"

Lost in Space

Since the 1960s, there have been close to 40 missions to Mars. Many different countries have launched these missions. Not all spacecraft make it to Mars. Others get there but are unable to send information back to Earth.

The earliest missions were flybys of the planet. These spacecraft took pictures of the planet and beamed them back to Earth. Later spacecraft orbited Mars. These orbit missions meant the spacecraft spent more time close to Mars. They sent back better pictures.

A Martian Mystery

In the summer of 1976, V*iking 1* and *2* were the first spacecraft to land on Mars. Their successful landing began a new era of Mars exploration.

Viking 1 and *2* could not move once they reached Mars's surface. However, they did take a picture that made many people wonder about life on Mars.

In one photo there appeared to be a human face. NASA scientists decided it was a natural rock formation that just happened to look like a face. But more eerie pictures were soon taken of Mars.

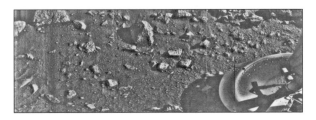

The first photograph ever taken from the surface of Mars by the *Viking I* lander, 1976.

Sojourner Success Story

On July 4, 1997, a US spacecraft called the *Pathfinder* landed on Mars. It opened its doors and released a small robot car or rover, called *Sojourner*.

Sojourner's mission was to roam the Martian surface and study rocks and dirt. Scientists believed that clues about life on Mars could be found in the rocks on the planet's surface.

When *Sojourner* finally made it to Mars, it did not send back any pictures of aliens. But it did send back the first in-depth information about the Martian surface.

NASA scientists controlled *Sojourner* by radio signals beamed from Earth. Every signal took 11 minutes to travel 93 million miles to Mars.

From the rocks *Sojourner* collected, scientists discovered that there was once water on the dry planet. On Earth, where there is water, there is life. This discovery of water traces on Mars helped prove that there might have been life on Mars some time in the past.

Martian Mystery

In July 1988, the USSR sent two landers called *Phobos I* and *Phobos II* to study Phobos. Phobos is one of the two moons that orbit Mars.

Phobos I shut down on its way to Mars. It was powered by solar panels. At some point, *Phobos I* got lost and pointed its panels away from the sun. The panels could not charge and it quickly lost power.

Phobos II seemed to do better. It stayed in contact with Earth until right before it was about to drop to the moon's surface. Then communications were lost. It is not known if *Phobos II* made it to Phobos' surface.

The last pictures *Phobos II* beamed back to Earth were amazing. There appeared to be a long dark object on the surface of Mars!

News reporters told the world of the strange images. Many people wondered if these images were alien buildings on Mars. People wondered if aliens could have shut down *Phobos I* and *II*.

Soviet scientists said that the image was actually the shadow of the moon, Phobos, on the Martian surface. Because Phobos is not perfectly round, and the surface of Mars is not flat, the shadow made a strange shape. Still, many UFO followers did not believe this explanation.

Mars Observer is Missing

When the US lander *Mars Observer* suddenly lost communications, scientists were puzzled. On August 22, 1993, the spacecraft prepared to orbit Mars. Without warning, its transmitters turned off. Scientists believe that there was a leak in the ship's steering systems and it lost control.

Since *Sojourner*'s success, there have been several more missions to Mars. Some have run into problems. Some, like the *Mars Odyssey* and the *Mars Global Surveyor* are successfully orbiting the planet. In January 2004, twin rovers *Spirit* and *Opportunity* roam across the Martian surface. The search for life on Mars continues.

Missions to Mars

There have been many missions to Mars in the last 40 years. Here are some of them. There are many more planned for the future.

Marsnik 1 and *2*—October 1960 USSR
Attempted Mars Flyby (Launch Failure)

Sputnik 22—October 1962 USSR
Attempted Mars Flyby

Mars 1—November 1962 USSR
Mars Flyby (Contact Lost)

Sputnik 24—November 1962 USSR
Attempted Mars Lander

Mariner 3 and *4*—November 1964 USA
Mars Flyby

Zond 2—November 1964 USSR
Mars Flyby (Contact Lost)

Mariner 6 and *7*—Summer 1969 USA
Mars Flyby

Mars 1969A and *B*—Spring 1969 USSR
Attempted Mars Orbiter (Launch Failure)

Mariner 8—May 1971 USA
Attempted Mars Flyby (Launch Failure)

Kosmos 419 — May 1971 USSR
Attempted Mars Orbiter/Lander

Mars 2 and *3* — May 1971 USSR
Mars Orbiter/Attempted Lander

Mariner 9 — May 1971 USA
Mars Orbiter

Mars 4, 5, 6, and *7* — Summer 1973 USSR
Mars Flyby, Orbiter, and Lander

Viking 1 and *2* — Summer 1975 USA
Mars Orbiter/Lander

Phobos I and *II* — July 1988 USSR
Attempted Mars Orbiter/Phobos Landers

Mars Observer — September 1992 USA
Attempted Mars Orbiter (Contact Lost)

Mars Global Surveyor — November 1996
USA Mars Orbiter

Mars 96 — November 1996 Russia
Attempted Mars Orbiter/Lander

Mars Pathfinder — December 1996 USA
Mars Lander/Rover

Nozomi (Planet-B) — July 1998 Japan
Mars Orbiter

Mars Climate Orbiter — December 1998
USA Attempted Mars Orbiter

Mars Polar Lander and *Deep Space 2* —
January 1999
USA Attempted Mars Lander

Mars Odyssey — April 2001 USA
Mars Orbiter

Mars Express — June 2003 USA
Mars Orbiter/Lander

Spirit and Opportunity — Summer 2003
USA Mars Rovers

Mars Reconnaissance Orbiter — August 2005
USA Mars Orbiter

Phoenix — Late 2007 USA
Small Mars Scout Lander

Netlanders — Late 2007 France
Mars Netlanders

Mars 2009 — Late 2009 USA
Mars Science Laboratory Rover

Mars 2011 — 2011 USA
Scout Mission

CHAPTER 4

Missing Treasure Found

DATAFILE

Timeline

1681

The *Santa Maria De La Consolación* leaves Peru filled with Inca treasure. It soon sinks.

1990s

Two brothers in Ecuador find *Santa Maria*'s lost treasure while walking on the beach.

Where is Santa Clara, Ecuador?

HERE

Key Terms

galleon—a Spanish sailing ship

Incas—an ancient group of people who lived in South America from 1200 to the 1500s

salvage—to rescue a ship, its crew, or cargo from a shipwreck

Viceroy of Peru—the Spanish governor of the land captured by the conquistadors

?

Did You Know?

In South America, the Spanish conquerors, such as Pizarro, Cortes, Orellana, and Cabeza de Vaca, were called *conquistadors*.

Missing Treasure Found

In 1681, a Spanish galleon called the *Santa Maria De La Consolació*n left Peru filled with Inca treasure. The ship traveled up the coast of South America to Panama. Captain Juan de Lerma had heard that pirates prowled the waters on the way to Panama. He wanted to delay his trip so he might avoid them. But the Viceroy of Peru ordered the ship to set sail. The treasure had to be in Panama before the Spanish fleet left for Spain. De Lerma followed his orders and set sail for Panama.

Off of the coast of Ecuador, a pirate ship under the command of Captain Sharpe attacked the *Santa Maria*. The attack was so bloody that to this day Ecuadorians call the nearby island of Santa Clara "El Muerto." This means "the dead."

The *Santa Maria*'s crew fought the pirates until the ship ran into a reef. Trapped, de Lerma ordered his men to burn the ship and protect the treasure. The ship went down full of treasure.

Captain Sharpe was so mad that he killed every man from the *Santa Maria* —350 in all. The shark infested waters made it impossible for Sharpe's men to get the treasure. It remained lost in its watery grave, forgotten.

Forgotten Fortune

In the 1990s, two brothers went for a walk along the beach of Santa Clara Island. One of them noticed a black stone rolling in the surf. He picked it up to look closer. He quickly realized that it was not a stone. It was a 300-year-old Spanish coin!

Word of the coin spread quickly. Roberto Aguirre, a wealthy businessman, set out to investigate which ship the coin had come from.

But the treasure hunt did not start in the ocean, it started in a library. Aguirre hired a professional treasure hunter named Joel Ruth. Ruth was an expert in coins and began searching for records of ships carrying this kind of coin. He found the *Santa Maria* story. From there he traced her location.

Scouring the Seas

For six years, Aguirre, Ruth, and a team of divers searched the ocean around Santa Clara. Divers found a trail of coins that stretched for miles on the ocean floor. The coins had been swept away from the ship by the current.

But as the divers got closer, they still could not find the wreck. Then one day, a local fisherman called for help. The fisherman told the divers that his net was caught on something in 30 feet of water. They went down to investigate and could not believe their eyes. Below them, under sand and seaweed, were large wooden beams. The beams were blackened from fire.

The divers collected samples of the wood to be tested. The tests showed that the wood was at least 370 years old. This was the same age as the *Santa Maria De La Consolación*.

Missing Treasure Lost Again?

The treasure aboard the *Santa Maria* was thought to be worth between $20 to $100 million dollars.

As far as the divers could tell, this wreck had never been discovered. This meant that all the treasure should still be on or near the ship.

The team of divers wanted to return to the wreck quickly. But when they returned, the wreck was gone. The ocean currents had covered the wood beams. The *Santa Maria* was once again hidden.

However, this time they knew where to look. The divers brought in high-powered water cannons to blow away the sand. Once again they uncovered the wreck. With the permission of the Ecuadorian government, the team began to salvage the wreck. They recovered coins, pottery, jewels, and gold. Most of all, they recovered the missing *Santa Maria De La Consolación*.

Spanish Treasure Fleets

After Columbus made his famous voyage to the new world in 1492, Spain became Europe's most powerful country. The Spanish navy was unbeatable for almost 100 years.

Spain established trade routes from conquered lands in Central and South America back to Spain. The Spanish ships brought goods from Europe to colonial settlers. They then brought back treasures from the New World.

These ships were known as treasure fleets, or *flotas* in Spanish. There were two main fleets: the *Tierra Firme* and the *Nueva España*. Each fleet was made up of many ships. The merchant ships carried the treasure. Smaller ships scouted for pirates. And large, heavily armed gun ships protected them all.

Spanish Conquistadors and the End of the Inca Empire

The Incas were an ancient people who ruled a large empire in South America. They ruled from their capital, which today is the city of Cuzco in Peru.

The Incas were religious. They worshiped the natural world, sun, and moon. They were great astronomers, and they built great cities and temples. They ruled their empire from 1200 to 1532, when the Spanish conquered their empire.

The Spanish explorer Pizarro came to the Inca rulers and asked them to become Christians. The Inca emperor, Atahuallpa, refused and was captured by the Spanish and killed. This began the destruction of the Inca Empire. Spain claimed the Inca's gold and silver treasures and sent them back to Spain.

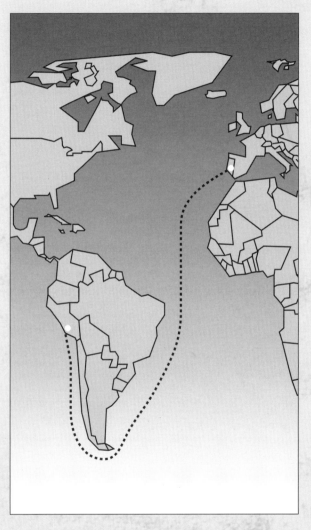

The Spanish conquistadors shipped the treasures they seized from South America back to Spain.

The Ivory-billed Woodpecker
DATAFILE

Timeline

1950s
The last ivory-billed woodpecker sighting.

April 1999
David Kulivan spots a male and female ivory-billed woodpecker in a Louisiana forest.

January 2002
A team of experts search for the ivory-billed woodpecker.

Where is Louisiana?

HERE▶

Key Terms

forestry—the study of caring for forests and forest wildlife

habitat—the special kind of area where a plant or an animal lives

skeptic—a person who doubts something until he or she sees proof

unique—one-of-a-kind or original

?

Did You Know?

Woodpeckers have *zygodactyl* feet. This means they have two toes pointing forward and two pointing backwards. These toes help them climb trees.

The Ivory-billed Woodpecker

The ivory-billed woodpecker is native to the southeast United States. That is, it lived there until the 1950s. At that time, bird watchers no longer spotted these unique birds.

The male ivory-billed woodpecker has a bright red crest on its head. The males and females both have long white bills. They use their bills to tear bark from dead trees. They then eat insect larva growing under the bark.

The ivory-billed woodpecker is America's largest woodpecker. The birds are 20 inches tall. Their wings are three feet from tip to tip. Their calls sound like a toy trumpet.

When years passed without any sightings of the ivory-billed woodpeckers, bird watchers believed they were extinct. Bird watchers believed hunting and logging of the bird's habitat had wiped out the bird. But in 1999, many bird watchers changed their minds.

A Walk in the Woods

In 1999, David Kulivan was a forestry student at Louisiana State University. On April Fool's Day, he decided to go turkey hunting. He set out for the Pearl River Wildlife Management Area near New Orleans. This forest covers 35,000 acres. It is filled with old trees and swamps.

As Kulivan walked through the forest, he spotted a pair of ivory-billed woodpeckers—a male and a female. His sighting was the first time anyone got a good look at the birds in nearly 50 years!

When Kulivan reported his sighting, many people did not believe him. But he gave a good description of the male's red crest, their white bills, and their unique call. Soon, the skeptics were convinced his sighting was real.

A Search Gets Started

In January 2002, three years after Kulivan's sighting, a search for the birds started. A German company called Zeiss paid for a research trip into the Pearl River Wildlife Management Area. The company organized a team of six top bird watchers from around the world.

The Zeiss team spent a month hiking through the forest and swamps looking for the birds. They looked up into the dead trees where the birds usually fed. They also looked for areas where they might nest. The used high-tech digital cameras and sound equipment to try to find the birds.

After searching for a month, the Zeiss team was not able to find the birds. But they did find signs of the ivory-billed woodpecker. They found possible nests and feeding areas.

Do They Exist?

Even though the Zeiss team did not find the birds, many people remain hopeful that the birds will be found. Bird watchers are thrilled at the idea that the ivory-billed woodpecker might exist. The ivory-billed woodpecker is a majestic bird. Many people think it is a symbol of America's natural beauty.

Woodpecker Stats

- The ivory-billed woodpecker is the largest woodpecker in North America.

- Ivory-billed woodpeckers can be from 19–21 inches in length.

- Ivory-billed woodpeckers build their nests in trees.

- Female ivory-billed woodpeckers usually lay up to three eggs at a time.

- Ivory-billed woodpeckers eat insect larvae that grow in hollow trees.

- Ivory-billed woodpeckers are solitary birds, and do not live in a flock.

- Ivory-billed woodpeckers do not spend much time in one place. They roam over large feeding territories.

The pileated woodpecker is a close relative of the ivory-billed woodpecker.

CHAPTER 6

Monet's Torrent de la Creuse
DATAFILE

Timeline

1872

French Impressionist artist Claude Monet creates the oil painting *Impression, Sunrise*.

1933

The Nazi party takes control of Germany and begins its efforts to eliminate "undesirables," including Jews and Gypsies. Their homes are looted and any items of value are stolen.

Where is France?

Key Terms

anonymous—not identified by name; of unknown name

concentration camps—places where large numbers of political prisoners or members of persecuted minorities are imprisoned

loot—goods, especially private property, taken from an enemy in war

?

Did You Know?

Claude Monet's heir gave the French Academy of Fine Arts Monet's estate at Giverny. In 1980, the estate opened for tourists around the world to enjoy and admire the gardens that inspired Monet's artwork.

Monet's Torrent de la Creuse

Claude Monet was a very famous French painter. His painting style was called Impressionism. Monet and other Impressionists usually painted out in the open air. Standing outside, they would paint landscapes very quickly. The point was to catch natural light before it changed.

A painting Monet did in 1872 was the first Impressionist artwork. *Impression, Sunrise* was painted with thick, bold brush strokes. It depicts a pinkish-orange sunrise over water. There's a boat out in the water and hazy shadows of buildings in the background.

Monet is especially known for paintings of water lilies, haystacks, and boats. His work appears in art museums all over the world. Claude Monet died in 1926. Today his paintings fetch millions of dollars.

During World War II, the Nazis sent millions of Jews to **concentration camps**. Many of them died there. Some died of disease or starvation. But many were executed. These mass killings were known as the Holocaust.

When the Nazis shipped Jews off to the camps, they looted their family possessions. Artworks and other valuables were plundered. In addition to art, things like china and silver were taken. Some of the plundered art was priceless. Stolen artworks included paintings by Monet and other famous artists. Much of the art was taken from Jewish families. A lot came from museums as well. About 20 percent of all the art in Europe was plundered by the Nazis.

Adolph Hitler planned to build a large art museum in his hometown of Linz, Austria. He wanted to keep all the world's greatest art treasures there. He was going to call it the Führermuseum. But fortunately, Hitler was defeated and the museum never came to be.

After the war, much of the art was recovered. The Allies found the artworks and tried to return them to their rightful owners.

There is a famous photo of Gen. Dwight D. Eisenhower in a German salt mine. He is surrounded by artwork stolen by the Nazis. Much of the stolen art was hidden in tunnels, salt mines, and castles.

Americans were largely responsible for returning the stolen art. However, many artworks have never been returned to their rightful owners.

Monet's *Torrent de la Creuse* is one example. This 1889 painting shows the Creuse River joining the Little Creuse River. The churning waters are painted in shades of green and blue.

Torrent de la Creuse disappeared in 1941, during World War II. It had been in a family bank vault in France. The missing Monet belonged to a man named Max Heilbronn. German soldiers raided the vault and took the painting. They took nine of Heilbronn's other paintings as well.

Today, Heilbronn's daughter is trying to get *Torrent de la Creuse* back. Ginette Heilbronn Moulin is in her eighties now. She is the chairwoman of the famous Galeries Lafayette department stores. Her grandson, Guillaume Houzé, is helping with the hunt.

Four of the 10 missing paintings have been found. One is a Renoir painting of roses. Ms. Moulin's family noticed the painting for sale at a Christie's auction in 2004.

Christie's is a famous auction house in London. It is the world's second-largest fine-art auction house. Sotheby's is the biggest. Paintings sell for millions of dollars at Christie's and Sotheby's. So the art world pays close attention to what is sold there.

Two of the other missing Heilbronn paintings are by Camille Pissarro. These two Impressionist landscapes were found in Hermann Goering's house in Berlin. Goering was Hitler's right-hand man.

Artworks have what is known as "provenance." This is a detailed record of who legally owned the work from the time it was created. The provenance shows each time it was sold and to whom. Without provenance, a painting or sculpture could be fake. Or it could be stolen.

Many of the works looted by the Nazis are missing information from the war years. From 1933 through 1945, the provenance records are unclear for many artworks.

Even today, 30,000 pieces of art are still missing. Jewish scholars and art historians are working to track them down.

A lot of the works with gaps in provenance are now in museums all over the world. For instance, the Metropolitan Museum of Art in New York put together a list of 393 paintings that had information missing from the World War II period.

Other museums have made similar lists. Museum officials are working to track down the missing information. So far, not many artworks have been proven to be Nazi loot.

Since the late 1980s, people have been more careful about provenance. Art dealers and museums don't want to own or sell art that might have been stolen.

Priceless paintings discovered among looted, stolen, and hidden art by American soldiers at the end of World War II.

The Wildenstein family has been selling art in France for five generations. Wildenstein and Company was founded in Paris in 1875. Today they are billionaire art dealers. There are Wildenstein galleries in New York, London, and Tokyo.

Ginette Heilbronn Moulin believes the Wildensteins know where her Monet is. She is suing them to find out.

In July 2011, Guy Wildenstein was charged with possessing 30 stolen or missing artworks. Police found them at the Wildenstein Institute's warehouse in Paris. Wildenstein, who is Jewish, denies that any of them are Nazi loot.

But the discovery of the 30 works aroused Ms. Moulin's suspicions.

The Wildensteins publish artwork lists that are respected by the art world. Scholars think of the catalogs as a reliable guide to who has which famous paintings. For instance, no art dealer would sell a Monet that's not listed in the Wildenstein guide.

The 1979 and 1996 Wildenstein guides include *Torrent de la Creuse*. The Monet list for those years shows the painting as belonging to a private collector. But it doesn't list the collector's name. The 1979 edition lists "an anonymous owner." The 1996 catalog lists "an unidentified American owner."

Guy Wildenstein claims there was a mistake in the catalog. Ms. Moulin thinks otherwise. She thinks the Wildensteins either have the missing Monet or know where it is.

Guy Wildenstein's father, Daniel Wildenstein, probably had the answers. But he died in 2001.

Daniel Wildenstein was a scholar world-famous for his knowledge of Impressionism. He was the one who created the Monet catalogs.

The Metropolitan Museum of Art has a Monet painting that is very similar to *Torrent de la Creuse*. The museum lists the painting as *Rapids on the Petite Creuse at Fresselines*. The Metropolitan Museum's gallery label says the painting is "nearly identical" to *Torrent de la Creuse*. It is not on display.

Records show the Wildensteins bought the "nearly identical" painting in 1958. They bought it from a private collector, then sold it to Adelaide Milton de Groot. She donated it to the Metropolitan Museum in 1967.

A Jewish group in New York questioned the Met about their "nearly identical" painting. The group is called the Conference on Jewish Material Claims Against Germany. It tries to help Holocaust survivors and their heirs get their property back.

A team of art historians and scholars is sifting through the evidence. They are trying to track down information about the missing Monet.

"This painting represents some of the history of our family," Ms. Moulin said. "It was my grandson who pushed me to react. He doesn't understand how this could happen."

Claude Monet, the son of a grocer, was born in Paris, France, in 1840. Monet always knew that he wanted to be an artist. He studied along with great artists like Manet, Renoir, and Sisley. Monet moved to the town of

Giverny in Normandy, France, in 1883. It was at Giverny where Monet painted his most famous series of paintings, his water lilies. One water lily painting sold for over $80 million in 2008. Monet died in 1926 at the age of 86.

Missing Planets
DATAFILE

Timeline

February 18, 1930

Clyde Tombaugh confirms the theory of a ninth
planet in our solar system with the discovery of
Pluto at the Lowell Observatory in Arizona.

August 2006

The International Astronomical Union announces
that Pluto will no longer be considered a planet
based on its new rules on what constitutes a planet.

Where is Arizona?

HERE

Key Terms

dwarf planet—celestial body resembling a small planet but lacking certain technical criteria that are required for it to be classed as such

NASA's Wide-field Infrared Survey Explorer (WISE)—the WISE is an infrared-wavelength astronomical space telescope launched on December 14, 2009

robotic—mechanical, relating to robots

?

Did You Know?

NASA's Wide-field Infrared Survey Explorer, or WISE, was launched in 2009. WISE surveyed the sky with infrared light. NASA released an image of the entire universe in the spring of 2012.

Missing Planets

People have always looked up at the night sky in wonder. What is out there?

Our solar system includes the Sun and the planets that revolve around it. The Sun is only one of billions of stars in the sky. Many of those stars have their own planets, too.

In the past few hundred years, astronomers have learned a lot. But there's still a lot more they don't know. For instance, how many planets does our solar system really have?

For the last 50-plus years, schools have taught that there are nine planets. They are Mercury, Venus, Earth, Mars, Jupiter, Saturn, Uranus, Neptune, and Pluto. That's in order from closest to the Sun to farthest away.

Try using the following sentence to remember the planets' order: My Very Educated Mother Just Served Us Nine Pizzas. The beginning letters are in the same order as the names of the planets.

However, many astronomers now say Pluto is not a planet. They say it is an icy body. It is one of 1,000 or so icy bodies. They form the Kuiper Belt, a group of icy bodies orbiting Earth. They are all farther away than Neptune, the farthest planet. These icy bodies are similar to comets.

Some astronomers still include Pluto as the last planet, however. They are upset that some people are saying Pluto is not a planet.

These astronomers admit things would be different if Pluto were discovered today. It probably would not be named as a planet. That's because it's so small and so different from the other planets.

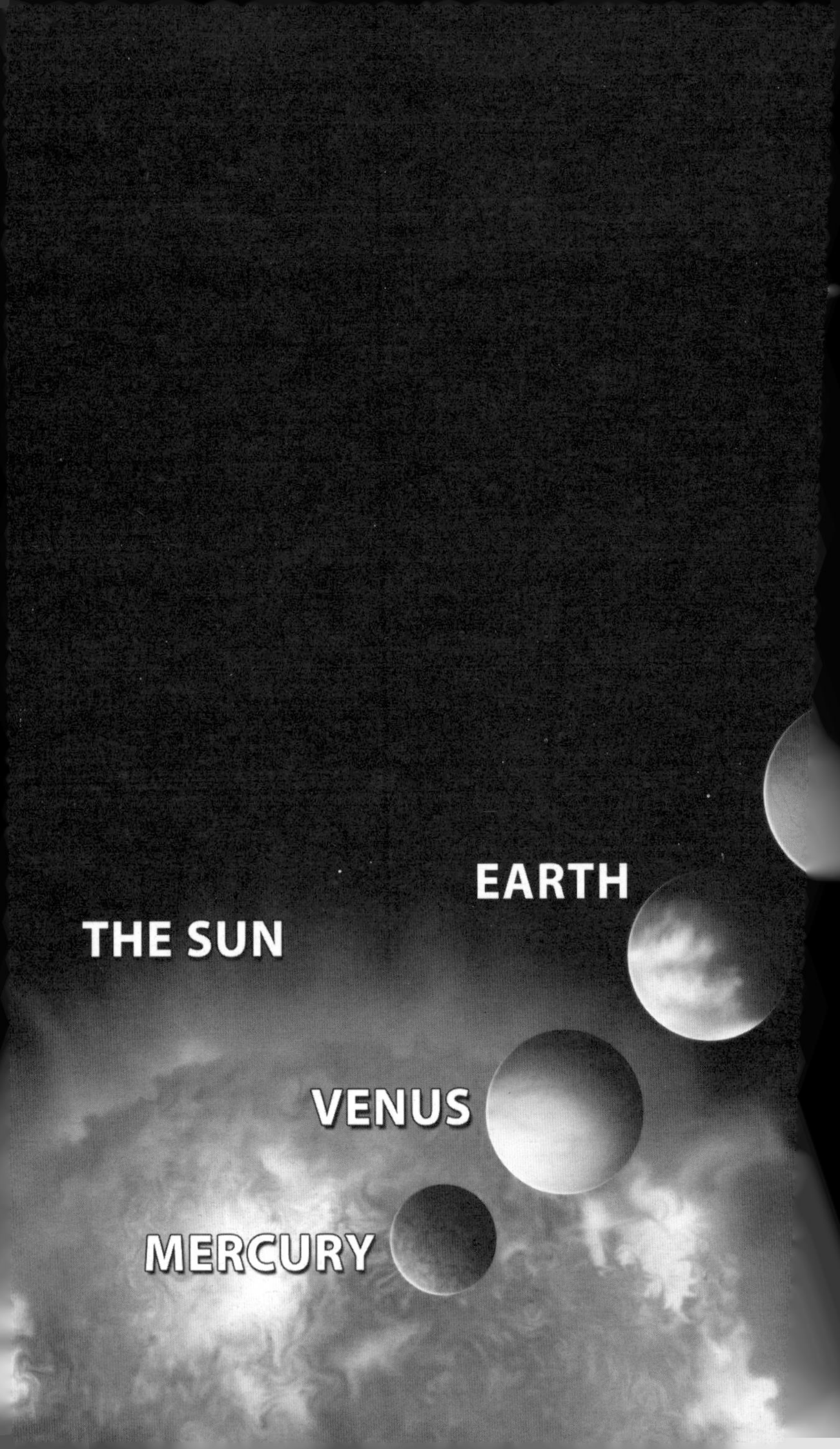
EARTH
THE SUN
VENUS
MERCURY

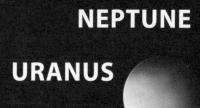

NEPTUNE

URANUS

SATURN

JUPITER

MARS

Pluto is only about 1,400 miles wide. That's less than half the width of the United States. It's smaller than Earth's moon. The icy planet Pluto was discovered in 1930.

In 1992, the rest of the Kuiper Belt was discovered. Scientists found about 70 icy bodies that have an orbit similar to Pluto's. They call these the Plutinos.

When you include Pluto as a planet, it is the tiniest one. But as part of the Kuiper Belt, it is the biggest.

Pluto is not the only "missing planet." It all depends on what you consider to be a planet.

The word *planet* comes from the Greek word for "wanderer." That's because planets travel, or wander, around our Sun. They follow orbits, or paths. Some planets have circular orbits. Others' orbits are elliptical. That's a circle lengthened into an oval shape.

There are many bodies other than planets circling our Sun. In addition to icy bodies, there are asteroids. These rocky bodies are pretty much the same as planets, only smaller.

In 1801, astronomers found Ceres. It was orbiting between Mars and Jupiter. They called it a planet for a short while. But they found that it's really small—only about 600 miles wide. That's less than half as large as Pluto. And Ceres is part of a whole ring of rocky bodies. So the astronomers decided to call it an asteroid instead.

Another "missing planet" is Eros. It was discovered in 1898. Eros is shaped a bit like a shoe. It is located near Mars.

Eros was one of the first bodies visited by an Earth spacecraft. A NASA ship orbited Eros in 2000. In 2001, the *NEAR Shoemaker* landed on Eros. The robotic space probe was unmanned. Its purpose was to study Eros and report back to Earth.

Another space body was discovered in 2005. Like Pluto, it is far away, past Neptune. Its name is very similar to Eros. Eris is considered a dwarf planet, and it is about the same size as Pluto. Because of this, it was at first called the tenth planet.

The discovery of Eris led scientists to redefine the word *planet.* The International Astronomical Union (IAU) decided in 2006 that Eris is a dwarf planet. So is Pluto, along with Ceres, Haumea, and Makemake.

The new definition for what is a planet has three requirements. A planet must be in orbit around the sun. A planet must have enough mass to form a sphere. And a planet must have "cleared the neighborhood" of its orbit. This means that Pluto cannot be a planet, because it shares its orbit with many other icy bodies.

Dwarf planets are not really planets. They are too small. So by that definition, we are back to eight planets in our solar system.

The first four planets in our solar system are relatively small. Mercury, Venus, Earth, and Mars are tiny compared to the next four. Jupiter, Saturn, Uranus, and Neptune are giants by comparison.

Jupiter is the biggest planet in the solar system. Its name is fitting. Jupiter was the king of the ancient Roman gods. The planet Jupiter is 2.5 times larger than all the other planets combined. It is about 11.2 times further across than Earth. In surface area, Jupiter is about 122 times larger than Earth.

In 2005, scientists in France came up with a new theory. They ran computer models of when our solar system was formed. They concluded that there might have been a fifth giant planet. It may have been as large as Neptune, which is 57 times larger than Earth.

In 1999, other scientists also proposed a giant planet. They named it Tyche (pronounced ty-kee). These scientists thought Tyche could be four times as big as Jupiter.

Today a number of scientists agree that the giant planet probably does exist. But so far no one has seen it.

Scientists say the four giant planets used to be much closer. But there were many crashes with asteroids and comets. The big planets may have even crashed into each other.

Because of all the bouncing around, Jupiter moved closer to the Sun. And the other three giant planets moved farther away. Then they were evenly spaced out and each had enough room.

For a computer model to mean anything, it has to give the same results more times than not. The scientists kept trying different versions. But they all came out wrong.

In one version, Earth and Mars crashed, wiping each other out. We know that didn't happen. Earth and Mars are both still here.

In a different version, one of the four giant planets crashed into another and went flying out into space. But we know that didn't happen, either. Jupiter, Saturn, Uranus, and Neptune are all still here.

The scientists needed to come up with a version that worked every time. So they tried it with a fifth giant planet.

In this version, the fifth giant planet crashed into Jupiter. That made it go flying off into space. It flew extremely fast—200,000 miles per hour!

The missing giant, if it exists, is very far away by now. Going that fast, it would be in the farthest reaches of our solar system. There's something out there called the Oort Cloud. That's where scientists think the giant planet could be hiding.

The Oort Cloud is a huge cloud of icy bodies. It is nearly a light-year away from the Sun. A light year is the distance a beam of light could travel in a year. Light travels at 186,282 miles per second! So that is very far away. In fact, it is about six trillion miles.

Scientists think the giant gas planet may be visible in the scans made by NASA's Wide-field Infrared Survey Explorer. The scans are all done. It just remains to look at all of them.

GLOSSARY

anonymous—not identified by name; of unknown name

astronomer—a scientist who studies Earth, planets, stars, and space

compass—a magnetic tool that points to the direction you are heading

concentration camps—places where large numbers of political prisoners or members of persecuted minorities are imprisoned

database—a computerized list of information

dwarf planet—celestial body resembling a small planet but lacking certain technical criteria that are required for it to be classed as such

federal—having to do with the US government

forestry—the study of caring for forests and forest wildlife

galleon—a Spanish sailing ship

habitat—the special kind of area where a plant or animal lives

Incas—an ancient group of people who lived in South America from 1200 to the 1500s

loot—goods, especially private property, taken from an enemy in war

magnetic north—the direction of Earth's magnetic north pole

NASA—National Aeronautics and Space Administration: the team that runs the US space program

NASA's Wide-field Infrared Survey Explorer (WISE)—the WISE is an infrared-wavelength astronomical space telescope launched on December 14, 2009

orbit—to move about something in a circular path

parole—a closely watched prisoner on release from jail

phenomenon—an amazing or hard to explain event

portal—a door or entrance; a way in or out

robotic—mechanical, relating to robots

salvage—to rescue a ship, its crew, or cargo from a shipwreck

skeptic—a person who doubts something until he or she sees proof

supernatural—beyond natural or scientific forces

telescope—an instrument for viewing distant objects by refracting light rays through a lens or the reflection of light rays by a concave mirror

terrorist—a person who tries to attack a country or group using violence

true north—the direction of the North Pole

unique—one-of-a-kind or original

vessels—boats, ships

Viceroy of Peru—the Spanish governor of the land captured by the conquistadors

Index